America Votes

How Our President Is Elected

Written *by* Linda Granfield
Illustrated *by* Steve Björkman

Kids Can Press

**For Madeleine Goebel
from a grateful grade-five student — L.G.**

**For the Peotter family with great appreciation
and respect — S.B.**

Acknowledgments
My sincerest gratitude goes to John Bell for his insights, generous
humor, and incredible patience during the editorial process. Thanks as well to
Rivka Cranley and the Kids Can Press crew; to Steve Björkman, whose artwork
brings zip to the pages; and to Cal, Brian, and Devon Smiley, who delivered party
support at all times. I also thank the many U.S. government departments, bureaus
and agencies, private organizations, and the members of the U.S. Congress;
they make voluminous amounts of material available to all citizens who
are interested in how our government works. And finally, thanks to the
many historians, biographers, journalists, and artists who, through two
centuries, have passionately chronicled American politics.

★ ★ ★

Text © 2003 Linda Granfield
Illustrations © 2003 Steve Björkman

Edited by John Bell
Designed by Julia Naimska
Printed in Hong Kong, China, by Wing King Tong
Company Limited

The hardcover edition of this book is smyth sewn
casebound.
The paperback edition of this book is limp sewn with a
drawn-on cover.

CM 03 0 9 8 7 6 5 4 3 2 1
CM PA 03 0 9 8 7 6 5 4 3 2 1

Kids Can Press acknowledges the financial support of the
Ontario Arts Council, the Canada Council for the Arts and
the Government of Canada, through the BPIDP, for our
publishing activity.

Published in Canada by
Kids Can Press Ltd.
29 Birch Avenue
Toronto, ON M4V 1E2

Published in the U.S. by
Kids Can Press Ltd.
2250 Military Road
Tonawanda, NY 14150

www.kidscanpress.com

National Library of Canada Cataloguing in Publication Data

Granfield, Linda
America votes : how our president is elected / written
by Linda Granfield ; illustrated by Steve Björkman.

Includes index.
ISBN 1-55337-086-4 (bound).   ISBN 1-55337-087-2 (pbk.)

1. Presidents — United States — Election — Juvenile
literature.
I. Björkman, Steve II. Title.

JK528.G73 2003   j324.6'3'0973   C2002-905335-8

Kids Can Press is a **Corus**™ Entertainment company

Contents

The Right to Vote — Your Right to Vote

As every November rolls around, signs of an election appear in your neighborhood, on TV, and in the newspapers. Your favorite sitcom is pre-empted by candidates' speeches and political ads. Oh no, you think, another election. Aren't they boring? Can't you just ignore them until you're an adult?

No! Elections aren't boring. They make lots of things happen all over the country for more than a year, and you can be part of the excitement. As you'll see, you don't have to wait until you're an adult to take part in elections. In a democracy like America's, people have the right and privilege to elect the men and women who will govern them. Your right to vote is protected by the Constitution of the United States — no one can deny you the right to vote because of your race, religious beliefs, or sex.

In America, we expect our elected officials to answer for their actions. We expect them to act responsibly on our behalf, whether we voted for them or not. And if they don't, we vote for someone else. Our right to vote is called *suffrage*, or our political *franchise*.

Not everyone on Earth has this protected right. In some countries, people are never asked to choose a new government. They are forced to accept whatever group seizes power. They can't vote a person out of office, so they must find other ways, such as protests and violence, to make their wishes known.

It's no fun feeling powerless and insecure. Between June and September 1988, the people of Haiti were ruled by three different governments, each one overthrowing the one before. Elections were held, but they weren't fair. Technically, the people had a say, but the leaders had decided beforehand who would win. Having real elections regularly sounds better, doesn't it?

You may have to wait until you are eighteen to vote in a local or national government election, but you may already vote in your home or classroom. Votes may determine where you go on the family vacation or who will be class president.

Learning about elections and voting makes each of us a powerful part of our communities and of the United States.

Get involved! Get your voice heard! Get ready to vote!

Winds of Change

The multiparty system with regular elections is how we choose a new government in the United States, but it's not the only way a country can decide on its leaders.

In a one-party system, all the candidates belong to the same party and have been approved by the leaders of that party. That doesn't leave people much of a choice. The Soviet Union, China, and many Eastern European countries had one-party systems for many years.

Throughout 1989 and 1990, people in these countries demanded multiparty systems. Their public demonstrations showed how important real choice in elections was to them. In Russia, Bulgaria, the Czech Republic, Hungary, Poland, and several other countries, the Communist Party is no longer the only party on the ballot.

The people of China were not successful in their quest for a democracy. The government crushed their protests in 1989. Many leaders of the movement were jailed. As of 2002, China remains a one-party nation where voters have little choice. But political situations can change quickly, and the voters of the world can generate a great deal of power.

★★★ 5

Who Can Vote?

Once you've turned eighteen, you'll be eligible to vote. What happens in American local and national governments is then up to you — and millions of other voters.

In the past, some Americans were denied the right to vote because of their poverty, ethnic origin, or sex. Today, you can vote if you are a citizen of the United States, live in the town or city where you want to vote, and are at least eighteen years old.

Not everyone who lives in the United States can vote. In most states, people who have been convicted of a serious crime lose their right to vote. Just because you're old enough to work at the local fast-food outlet and pay taxes on your income or purchases doesn't mean you automatically get to vote. You must meet the age, citizenship, and residency requirements, too. (Hmmm. Is that "taxation without representation"?)

If you're enthusiastic about politics and elections, don't let your age keep you from getting involved in the electoral process. You can deliver flyers, post signs, help people get to the polling places on Election Day, attend and help organize rallies, or simply wear a button for the candidate you *would* vote for.

Hang in there! After your eighteenth birthday party, you'll have your say and the right to vote — it's guaranteed by our Constitution.

Some Important Dates

Since the United States of America became a nation, there have been many changes concerning voter eligibility.

1776 — The thirteen original United States declare that they're independent from Great Britain.

1776–81 — By passing the Articles of Confederation, the states form a "perpetual union." Each state's government sends delegates to a national Congress, where each of the thirteen states gets one vote.

1787–89 — The states make a "more perfect union" by adopting the U.S. Constitution. The new government has a president, a Congress, and a Supreme Court. (We still govern ourselves by this system.)

1790s — Most states require men to have a certain amount of wealth to be eligible to vote. New Jersey law even lets unmarried women who own enough property vote in some elections. (But we don't know if any of them did.)

1830s — By this time, most states have enacted laws that allow all white men to vote, no matter how little money they have. Many of these laws bar black men and all women from voting, no matter how much money they have.

1870 — The Fifteenth Amendment grants voting rights to all men "regardless of race, color, or previous condition of servitude." No longer can only white men who own property or run a business vote.

1877 — With the end of Reconstruction, the U.S. government stops enforcing the Fifteenth Amendment in the South. Many blacks once again lose the ability to vote.

1920 — The Nineteenth Amendment gives women the vote.

1961 — The Twenty-Third Amendment lets people in the District of Columbia vote for president but not for Congressional representation.

1971 — The Twenty-Sixth Amendment gives people eighteen and older the right to vote. Before that, the legal voting age was twenty-one. People argued that if eighteen-year-olds were mature enough to fight for their country, they should be able to vote.

"We Insist..."

When the U.S. Constitution went into effect over two hundred years ago, the "right to vote" didn't apply to most Americans. In fact, it took well over a century before federal elections were open to the half of adult citizens who happened to be female.

Even though women were not allowed to vote in the early 1800s, many were active in politics. Women helped to organize and lead the movements for abolition (ending slavery) and temperance (reducing the amount of alcohol people drank). Female activists began to feel frustrated that they could not contribute to these movements by voting. In fact, they could not even participate in some international abolitionist meetings. American activists Lucretia Mott and Elizabeth Cady Stanton met in London, England, while waiting for their husbands during an abolition conference.

In 1848, the first women's rights convention in the United States was held in Seneca Falls, New York. During two July days, a document called the "Declaration of Sentiments" was written, adopted, and signed by over one hundred men and women who acknowledged that women were being deprived of their rights, including their right to vote. "We insist," they wrote. They wanted this inequality between men and women stopped immediately, but their battle for the right to vote was to last seventy-two years.

Women who spoke out and fought for the right to vote were called *suffragettes*. Suffragettes and their supporters held meetings all over the world. The result? Riots, arrests, imprisonment, hunger strikes, and, for some, death.

After the American Civil War ended in 1865, and slavery was abolished, women's political rights became a heated issue. In 1869, the Wyoming Territory granted women equal suffrage. They could vote, hold state office, and serve on juries. But the rest of America's women were still struggling. In 1877, the women's suffrage amendment was first introduced to Congress.

Not all women *wanted* to vote. Some of them agreed with the men who thought that women were less intelligent and less able to make political decisions. Some opponents thought that women were too morally pure to get involved with politics. Others feared that voting women would become neglectful mothers and waste time at meetings. Cartoonists showed suffragettes as ugly, sinister women battling men with their placards and banners. Activists formed groups such as the National Association Opposed to Woman Suffrage.

During World War I, however, Americans saw the important contributions women made to the war cause. Thousands of men left their jobs and went to Europe to fight. That left women with extra responsibilities. They had to keep their homes and families going, *and* they had to work outside the home. Maybe women *did* deserve a say in how the government worked. Opinions began to change.

"MILK, SUGAR, OR LEMON?"

Wealthy socialite Alva Vanderbilt Belmont supported the women's suffrage movement by donating plenty of funds to the organizers. She also hosted rallies in her Chinese Tea House built overlooking the sea at her summer "cottage" — actually a mansion called Marble House in Newport, Rhode Island.

Belmont even commissioned a new set of china to show her support. Each white cup and saucer was decorated with blue lettering that proclaimed "Votes for Women." The tea drinkers were reminded why they were at Marble House every time they took a sip!

Voices Finally Heard

Years of suffragette parades and public speaking kept the right-to-vote issue in newspapers and magazines. Supporters used comic postcards and other items to promote their cause.

In 1919, after World War I had ended, advocates of women's suffrage built a fire in front of the White House to capture the attention of President Woodrow Wilson and the nation. They collected their firewood from historic battlefields, such as Brandywine. The plan was that the fire would burn from New Year's Day until the passage of the Nineteenth Amendment.

The police arrested some of the bonfire builders. But every time the authorities or the rain put the fire out, the suffragettes lit it again. By the end of January, the president pressured Congress to approve the amendment — and they did. On August 26, 1920, the Nineteenth Amendment was ratified. Women could vote at long last.

VOICES THAT ECHO STILL

From the earliest days of the struggle, men like abolitionist Frederick Douglass supported the women's vote issue. But the leaders of the movement were women. In the days before radio and TV, they used their speeches and articles to inform, challenge, and educate. Many of these activists died long before the Nineteenth Amendment was passed. They never got to vote, despite years of effort. But they helped bring about the chance for every woman in the United States to take part in shaping the country's government.

Lucretia Mott (1793–1880)
Lucretia and James Mott were abolitionists who helped found the American Anti-Slavery Society in 1833. Their home became a refuge for escaped slaves before the Civil War. The couple went to England for the World Anti-Slavery Convention, but women were not allowed to take part. Lucretia met another female abolitionist left out of this meeting, Elizabeth Cady Stanton. Years later, in 1848, they and other friends called the first women's rights convention in Seneca Falls.

Elizabeth Cady Stanton (1815–1902)

Elizabeth Cady was born in Johnstown, New York. In 1840, she married Henry Stanton, a lawyer and journalist who shared her anti-slavery views. Together, they raised a family, worked as abolitionists, and became supporters of women's rights. Stanton was one of the organizers of the 1848 convention at Seneca Falls and wrote speeches for both herself and Susan B. Anthony during the years of campaigning for the vote. Stanton was the first president of the National Woman Suffrage Association (NAWSA).

Amelia Bloomer (1818–1894)

Bloomer published a monthly temperance paper, *The Lily*, which brought Stanton's articles to a greater public than her speeches could reach. Bloomer's paper also provided information about less restrictive clothing for women, whose long skirts of five yards of fabric hindered their movements. One item of apparel described in the paper was a shorter, split skirt, later called "bloomers." But Amelia Bloomer did not invent the design.

Susan B. Anthony (1820–1906)

Susan Brownell Anthony was born in Adams, Massachusetts, and grew up to become a teacher in New York. Before the Civil War, she worked for the American Anti-Slavery Society. After the war, she wanted women to have the same rights black men were given under the Fourteenth and Fifteenth Amendments. Anthony was not at the Seneca Falls convention, but much later, in 1872, she tested the Fourteenth Amendment by voting in the presidential election. She was arrested and fined, but she never paid what she called an "unjust penalty." The case motivated her to further dedicate her life to gaining equal rights for women.

You *Can* Vote, but *You* Can't ...

Before the Civil War, some northern states allowed some free African-American men to vote, but the vast majority of voters were white men. After the war ended, the states passed the Fifteenth Amendment to the Constitution in 1870. This amendment said that the vote would not be denied on the basis of race, color, or past enslavement. It was written specifically to let black men vote.

But many politicians who had been in power in the South before the war did not want African-Americans to vote. They feared that the black voters would outnumber the white voters. To "protect" themselves from this, they gradually created the "Jim Crow" system, named after a character in a song-and-dance show. Special poll taxes, literacy tests (with trick questions), and land ownership requirements that state leaders knew many African-American men couldn't meet were mandatory. Threats and violence kept others from voting. By the early 1900s, as a result of all these actions, there were few African-Americans in the nation's legislatures, and white male voters continued to dominate U.S. politics.

The service of African-Americans during World War II, and the sight of what Nazi racism produced in Europe, made many Americans rethink their "separate but equal" attitudes. Throughout the 1940s the National Association for the Advancement of Colored People (NAACP) fought in the courts for integration and equal treatment. But African-Americans still had trouble registering to vote in the 1964 presidential election in some parts of the South. Nonviolent demonstrations, marches, and sit-ins became common as African-Americans and their supporters continued to struggle for their Constitutional rights. People were murdered for helping African-Americans register to vote. This violence sickened many Americans and contributed to the greater changes to come.

The Voting Rights Act of 1965

President Lyndon B. Johnson worked hard to make changes in America's civil rights policies. The Twenty-Fourth Amendment, which outlawed poll taxes, was passed in 1964. The Civil Rights Act of 1964 gave African-Americans equal access to public places and jobs.

But these actions weren't enough. In March 1965, Dr. Martin Luther King, Jr., led a march in Alabama from Selma to Montgomery to call attention to how the state was still keeping African-Americans from voting. Public protests and political discussion led President Johnson to send the Voting Rights bill to Congress. The Voting Rights Act was signed into law within a few months. It gave the federal government the power to watch over voter registration and elections where states had prevented people from voting. If states continued to discriminate against African-Americans (or those who could not speak English), federal examiners would be sent in to replace the local officials.

A quarter of a million new African-American voters were registered within months of the Act's passage. Amendments to the Act in 1970, 1975, and 1982 have extended its provisions. Today, African-American men and women serve at almost all levels of state and federal governments.

Say It Louder, Please!

When our forefathers voted (remember, only men could vote), many had to call the name of their choice *out loud* in front of the candidates and all of their supporters. This method of voting was called *viva voce*, Latin for voting "out loud."

Because all voting was public, there were many opportunities for bullying and vote buying. Merchants might say to customers who owed them money, "Vote for my candidate and we'll forgive this debt." Or a candidate's supporters might try to buy votes by purchasing drinks for voters. Whiskey was a cheap bribe — a gallon could buy a lot of votes. Fights sometimes erupted when drunken voters changed their minds at the last moment and supported candidates they hadn't been behind during the campaigning.

Some people thought voters should choose according to their consciences, not outside pressure. They pushed for secret ballots. Other people thought that voting in secret was sneaky. If you were committed to a candidate, they argued, why not proudly call out his name

in front of the community?

By the late 1800s, all Americans got secret paper ballots, also called *Australian ballots* (or "kangaroo voting") because the Australians had used them since 1856. New York was the first state to adopt the paper ballot for its state elections in 1889. In 1892, Grover Cleveland was the first U.S. president elected by secret ballot.

Today, most voters go into booths, or behind curtains or screens, so that no one can see how they mark their ballots.

Ballot is from the Italian word *ballotta*, meaning a round bullet. In the 1500s, in Venice, Italy, men voted by dropping a bullet-like ball into a box or urn marked with their candidate's name.

KIDS VOTING USA

Students under eighteen cannot legally vote, but many states give them a chance to cast a ballot, similar to the official one, through the nonpartisan organization Kids Voting USA. (A nonpartisan organization is not affiliated with any party.)

The Kids Voting program is operated by communities and schools. Students in kindergarten through grade twelve learn about the election process. On Election Day, younger students accompany their parents or a guardian to a polling place. While their parents cast official ballots, the students get to vote for *their* choice of candidate in the special Kids Voting polling booth. (High school students can go to vote on their own.) Statistics show that the Kids Voting program actually increases *parent* voter turnout by nearly five percent.

In 2000, the Kids Voting USA national results showed that students supported the winner of the election, George W. Bush, with 50.7 percent of their votes. (In the "adult election," Bush's opponent, Al Gore, was the popular winner — but check out the electoral college on page 28.) Perhaps all fifty states will be taking part in Kids Voting USA for the 2004 election.

Wanted: A Few Good Ballots

Today, you don't vote by dropping metal balls into a ballot box. There are many other ways you might record your choice instead. In fact, there is no single form of ballot used in every state. When you go to vote on Election Day, you'll find one of the following ballots waiting for you.

Paper ballot — Mark your choice of candidates with a pencil. Only about two percent of the registered voters in the United States were still using paper ballots in 1996.

Voting machine — Step inside the machine and close the curtain for privacy. Find the candidates' names under small levers or switches, and pull down the levers for your choices. Pull another lever to record your vote and open the curtain as you leave. Now there are also electronic voting machines. On these, you push buttons or touch the screen next to your candidates' names, like using a bank's cash machine. (Some models have a keyboard for typing in other names.)

Punchcard ballot — Take a card from an election worker. In the voting booth, punch out the holes in the card that match your choice of candidates. On some cards, the candidates' names are printed next to the holes. Other punchcards show only numbers, and you have to look up the list of corresponding candidates in a separate booklet.

Optical scan ballot — Draw an arrow or fill in a space on a paper ballot to select your candidate. In some systems, you can then put your ballot under a scanner to see if

you've made any mistakes. To count ballots, election workers feed each card through the same sort of optical scanner, which reads the markings and tabulates the votes right away.

There are advantages and disadvantages to the various types of ballots. Some prevent you from *overvoting*, or marking more than one choice for each office. Some let you *write in* the name of a new candidate if you don't like anyone on the official ballot. Some make the counting faster or more accurate.

No matter which kind of ballot device you've used, when you come away from the polling place, you should feel that you've had the chance to select your candidates secretly and that your vote will be counted.

WHAT A CHAD, CHAD STORY!

After the 2000 election, the United States was pushed to the brink of a Constitutional crisis. Why? Because the vote was so close, the result depended on which candidate had won in Florida. And thousands of punchcard ballots came out of Florida's voting booths without clean punch marks. How tabulators counted those ballots could determine who had won the presidency.

Suddenly, the word "chad" was everywhere. A chad is the tiny bit you punch out of paper with a hole-punch, or a voting instrument. The punchcard ballots had different kinds of chads. There were *pregnant* chads (bulging but with every corner still attached) and *swinging-door* chads (attached by two corners), and *hanging* chads (attached by one corner). How could tabulators tell how a voter had really meant to vote?

The bits of punched paper that fell on the floor were called *dead* chads. After the election recounts, some of those were sold as souvenirs. Meanwhile, politicians and the public alike argued for a better way to vote. Florida passed a bill to replace the infamous punchcards with new voting machines that are more accurate — and won't produce chads.

"One, Two, Three, Four ..."

REARDON | PEREZ | CHEN

On Election Day, polling places usually close to voters at 8 P.M. But different time zones across the United States mean that when voters in New York can no longer enter their polling places, Californians still have three hours of voting time.

The doors may be locked to voters, but the officials inside don't stop working. They still have to seal the machines or ballot boxes and send them, along with unused ballots and all the necessary paperwork, to where the votes will be counted.

Some tiny communities have only a few dozen ballots at the end of the day. Others have thousands, with more arriving by mail. Counting, and sometimes recounting, can take a few minutes per precinct, or hours. There may be *spoiled ballots* that were marked incorrectly and are uncountable. Or *undervotes*, where the ballot wasn't marked for every race. Or *overvotes*,

ballots marked more than once and, again, uncountable.

While election workers tabulate votes, TV and newspaper reporters keep up with the numbers. Newscasters also use *exit polls*, surveys of voters as they leave the polling places, to get a hint of the election outcome.

Sometimes, the media are in too much of a hurry to announce the winner of a presidential election. Faulty reporting in 1948 resulted in the headline "Dewey Defeats Truman." The *Chicago Tribune* told readers that Thomas E.

Dewey (the candidate the paper supported) had won the election. But Harry S. Truman was the actual winner.

In 2000, TV reporters spoke too soon about the state of Florida — twice. Based on exit polls, they first announced that Al Gore had won Florida's electoral votes. Then, based on a partial vote count, they reported that George W. Bush had won. Later, long past midnight, they announced that the state vote was too close to call. That night, no one knew who the next president of the United States would be.

"And *Again*, One, Two, Three ..."

When the vote count is very close, the losing candidate may ask for a recount. In some states, the law requires a recount if the race is close enough. With so many votes, a lot of mistakes can happen. Sometimes, tabulators find ballots that they never counted, or counted twice. Or someone added the totals wrong.

Recounts take time and money. There's a limit on the number of times candidates can ask for recounts if the results keep coming out the same. A count is official when the appropriate election official *certifies* the vote.

UNDERWATER AND UNDER THE WEATHER

Voters can find themselves in some strange situations on Election Day. Imagine that your doctor says your tonsils have to come out, and the best day for the operation is, you guessed it, Election Day! Don't worry — you can still vote. Or imagine that your brother is aboard a Navy submarine and will be at sea on Election Day. Can he still vote? He sure can — even if he's underwater.

Absentee ballots give every registered voter a chance to vote. Every state sets its own deadlines for voters to request and return completed ballots by mail. Oregon encourages all citizens to vote by mail, even if they'll be in town on Election Day. Officials there believe that mail-in ballots encourage more people to vote, with more careful thought. On the other hand, when you vote from home, other people may see your ballot or try to influence your vote.

Practice, Practice, Practice!

The word *candidate* comes from a Latin word meaning "clothed in white." Why? Long ago in ancient Rome, men who wished to be elected or appointed to office wore white gowns called togas. Imagine if modern-day candidates dressed in white togas for their TV debates!

This book concentrates on the presidential elections in the United States, but as a newly registered voter, you have other opportunities to vote people into (or out of) office. You may be approached by party members and asked to post an election sign on your lawn. You may also be asked to distribute election pamphlets, to hang up posters printed in different languages, or to walk with a candidate as she visits your neighborhood. Maybe you'll decide to volunteer at the local campaign headquarters, stuffing envelopes, or entering information into a computer.

Depending on the year, you might vote for the governor, the chief executive of your state, and for members of the state legislature. Depending on where you live, you might be able to vote for other officials, such as the lieutenant governor, the attorney general, and the treasurer. Some states have voters decide who will be the judges in the courts, rather than having the governor appoint them.

VOTE FOR ME. I'LL MAKE THE BEST DOGCATCHER.

VOTE FOR ME. I KNOW DOGS.

WHAT DO YOU THINK?

A *referendum* is a different kind of election, with no candidates. Instead, it's a chance for voters to decide an important public question. In fact, sometimes it's actually called a *question*, or a *proposition*. For example, in a city election, citizens might vote on the referendum issue of whether to allow skateboarding on sidewalks.

In some parts of the country, propositions can number in the hundreds. In other areas, there may be only a few questions for voters to consider. In some states, the voters' decision on a referendum means the law is immediately changed. In others, lawmakers may change the law after they consider what the majority of voters want and whether a new law would violate the state's constitution.

You've probably heard your parents talking about some of the other local officials who are elected — people such as school committee members who help decide how schools in your area will be run, or the mayor, who is the "governor" of your city or town. Maybe your vote is needed to elect a sheriff, or a dogcatcher!

Think of each of these elections as a chance for you to practice your listening and questioning skills at meetings or at your door when a candidate knocks. You'll get used to going to your polling place and making your mark on a ballot.

Get on the List!

Suppose you want to take swimming lessons. Or maybe you enjoy music, and you'd like to learn to play the guitar. If you sign up for an after-school class in either of these subjects, you'll probably have to register beforehand. The registration process lets the school check if you're eligible to take the classes, and ensures that you don't sign up for two classes at the same time.

There are similar reasons why you must register to vote. When you show up on Election Day, election workers will know that you are eligible to vote and will also make sure that you don't vote twice in the same election.

Voter registration is an easy process, but the requirements, locations, and deadlines for registration vary from state to state. The forms you need are available from local election officials in your city or county. Some registration locations may be at armed forces recruitment offices, motor vehicle offices, and public libraries. Often, you'll find them at post offices,

unemployment offices, public high schools, and universities. Registration outreach programs, sponsored by groups such as the League of Women Voters, can help you find a registration location.

You may register as a member of any political party, or say you are independent. On the form, you write your name, address, and date of birth (you sometimes need a birth certificate for proof). The forms have been translated into Spanish, Chinese, Japanese, Vietnamese, and Tagalog (Filipino) to help more people register to vote.

There's always a deadline for registering. You'll have to check with your local officials because the deadlines can be anywhere from ten to thirty days before an election. On Election Day, your name will be checked off the list of registered voters at the polling place.

So Who Actually Votes?

People sometimes complain that the government doesn't give them a chance to change what they don't like. But not all the people who have the right to vote use that right. What a waste!

★ In 2000, more than 105 million Americans voted in the presidential election. That sounds like a lot of people, but it's only 67.5 percent of all registered voters. And that's only 51 percent of all Americans who are eligible to vote. When *you* register to vote, you might want to invite an eligible *un*registered voter in your family to go with you and make it an event to celebrate!

★ Only 32.4 percent of people eighteen to twenty-four years old voted in the 1996 presidential election. Lack of interest in elections disturbs political organizers. They ask entertainers to promote voting to young people and set up Web sites to educate and encourage young voters. For the 2000 election, World Wrestling Entertainment organized the "Smackdown Your Vote" campaign, and MTV ran the "Choose or Lose" campaign.

★ Women traditionally make up about 53 percent of eligible voters. This statistic makes candidates pay attention to issues, such as subsidized child care, that are of special interest to women voters.

★ *Swing voters* account for 38 percent of American voters. They do not consider themselves supporters of one political party and often decide whom to vote for at the last moment. For a candidate, swing voters can mean the difference between winning and losing.

★ How do we measure up against voters in other countries? In 1993, a whopping 97.6 percent of registered voters turned out to vote in the presidential election in Azerbaijan. Wow!

Your Representatives in Congress

In 1787, the makers of the Constitution created a Congress of two "houses" to represent the American people. Voters would elect members of the House of Representatives every two years. Senators would be selected by their state legislatures every six years. That's how the government worked until 1913, when the Seventeenth Amendment made the voters of each state responsible for electing senators, as well as congressional representatives.

Congress is the legislative branch of our government, equal in power to the executive branch (the president) and the judicial branch (the Supreme Court and other courts). Congress makes our laws, decides the national budget, and figures out the taxes that will give America its "spending money."

Elections for Congress are held in November, just like the presidential elections. Unlike the president, representatives and senators can serve as long

as they are elected and re-elected. Every two years, one-third of the Senate and the whole House of Representatives must stand for election. Sometimes, the six- and two-year rotations mean that senators and representatives are running at the same time as the presidential candidates. Talk about opportunities to vote!

Each state sends two senators to Washington. All voters in a state may vote for senators. Since 1911, the size of

the House of Representatives has been limited to 435. The number of representatives sent from each state depends on the population of the state. Only the voters living in the congressional district the candidate will represent can elect that representative.

Every ten years, the U.S. Census Bureau counts America's population, divides the result by the number of representatives' seats (435), and distributes those seats to the states so that all districts will be about the same size. This means that for the next ten years, a state may have more or fewer representatives than it did before. State legislatures must redraw the boundaries of each state's congressional districts to guarantee fair, equal representation throughout the state.

CATCH THAT GERRYMANDER!

Every party tries to draw election districts to make sure more of its candidates get elected. Party A might draw a district on the map that winds and twists far enough to include more of its known supporters. Or Party B may change the boundaries so that most of Party A's voters are in one district. That way, Party A will win the district, but Party B will win the rest of the state.

Drawing a strangely shaped district to benefit your own political party is called "gerrymandering," named for Elbridge Gerry, who was the Democratic-Republican governor of Massachusetts in 1812 when a famous case of redrawn districts was in the news.

While Gerry was in office, the boundaries of some electoral districts were redrawn so that his party was sure to win. On the map, the lines of the new boundary formed the shape of a salamander's body. An opposing, Federalist newspaper said it should be called a "gerrymander." The new word was not meant as a compliment to Governor Gerry.

You might be accused of gerrymandering on your next birthday if you're seen cutting around those icing roses to make sure your best friend gets plenty of them. Beware!

What Does the President Do?

The president of the United States is a busy person. Most of his duties fall into these three "chief" areas.

★ As *chief executive*, the president is in charge of assuring that U.S. laws are executed. The president may also propose new laws to Congress.

★ As *commander in chief*, the president is in charge of America's military forces. He commands the Army, Navy, and Air Force in times of both war and peace.

The "job" of president of the United States can look like a lot of fun. And it is, sometimes — there are celebrities to meet, huge state dinners to host, White House events such as the annual Easter Egg Roll to enjoy with children, and lots of travel to interesting places. The White House, where the president and his family live, has its own bowling alley, movie theater, and swimming pool. Ever imagine having your own airplane? The president flies around the world aboard Air Force One.

But for every fun time, there are occasions when the president has to deliver important speeches or listen to criticism from unhappy voters. He spends long nights talking to advisers when something goes wrong. He is "on call" twenty-four hours a day. He is often away from his family, surrounded instead by aides and security personnel, and doing business, not sightseeing. Being the president is not an easy job, but it can bring a great deal of personal satisfaction.

★ As *chief of state*, the president represents America to other countries around the world. He meets with other world leaders and makes agreements with them on, for example, international business, arms control, and environmental issues.

Who Can Be President?

Not just anyone who is interested in the office can be president of the United States. According to the Constitution, a person must meet three conditions first. A president must

1. be a citizen who was *born* in the United States
2. have lived in the United States for fourteen years
3. be at least 35 years old

Think about these three conditions and why they are important. If a candidate was born in the United States, she has been raised in our culture. By age thirty-five, this American has been established in some business or political position. Her experience has made her wise about life and knowledgeable about our nation — a level of maturity that can help her take on the duties of president.

What about a person who comes to the United States as a young child and grows up to be an accomplished, mature American? She would still be unable to become president because she was born in another country.

How Long Can a President Serve?

George Washington served two terms as president and then retired to Mount Vernon, his farm in Virginia. No presidents after Washington served for more than eight years until Franklin D. Roosevelt — he decided to run for a third term in 1940. World War II was raging, and Roosevelt believed that wartime was not a good time to change leadership. Voters agreed and elected Roosevelt to a third term — and then a fourth. Unfortunately, he died before the war was over.

In 1951, Congress and the states passed the Twenty-Second Amendment that says no president can be elected for more than two terms. After two terms, a new president has a chance to bring fresh ideas and renewed energy to the office and the nation.

No College Degrees Given Here!

When you mark your ballot on Election Day, you're not voting *directly* for the next president. Instead, you're voting for your state's *electors* — people who will choose the president.

The *electoral college* was written into the Constitution in 1787. Under this system, each state has as many electoral votes as it has senators and representatives in Congress. Over more than two centuries, the system has been modified only slightly. The District of Columbia now chooses three electors, as many as the smallest state. But there are no electoral votes for U.S. territories, such as Guam.

How do you get to be an elector? Each party assembles a list, or *slate*, of candidates for this task. Political leaders like to nominate people who have given loyal service to their party. In some states, your name as a nominee would appear on the ballot, right below your party's candidate for president. But in many states, you and other electors would be invisible to voters.

By law, electors in most states can vote for anybody they want, even someone who isn't on the ballot. But usually they vote for their party's candidate. In most states, whichever candidate wins most of the people's vote — known as the *popular vote* — wins *all* the electoral votes. A candidate can win 49 percent of the popular vote in a state and still get *no* electors' votes. But when all the electors' votes in all the states are totaled, the electoral college can turn a candidate's slight lead in the popular vote into a clear victory — and a big lead into a *landslide*, or overwhelming win.

After Election Day, electors in each state meet on the first Monday after the second Wednesday in December to cast their votes for the president and vice president. The states send their official packages of electoral votes to the federal government, to arrive by a specified date in December.

In early January, the electoral votes are counted with the new Senate and the House of Representatives watching, and the vice president in charge. Each state's votes are examined and read aloud in alphabetical order. The winner is decided by an absolute majority of electors, or half of the total votes plus one (270 out of 538). The winners take the oath of office two weeks later, on January 20.

Some "College Highlights"

The electoral college has gone through some crises, turning elections into raging arguments over who really won. In 1800 and 1824, no candidate won an absolute majority in the electoral college, so the House of Representatives chose the president. In 1876, the political parties disputed the winner in three crucial states, and a special commission chose the president. And in 1888 and 2000, the candidate who won the most popular votes didn't win the most electoral votes and, therefore, didn't become president.

Results like these have made many people unhappy with the electoral college. Over the last two centuries, more than seven hundred proposals were introduced in Congress to reform or eliminate it. But only a Constitutional amendment can change our system. That means two-thirds of the states must agree, including many small states that get extra power from the electoral college.

There are fifty states in all, but what's the smallest number that a candidate can win and still gain a majority in the electoral college? The answer may surprise you. Right now if a candidate wins just the eleven largest states, he collects 271 electors' votes, enough to become president.

Let's Have a Party

What do you think of when you hear the word "party"? Balloons, fantastic food, music and friends? You can find all of these things during an election, but you'll also find other kinds of parties — *political* parties.

The U.S. Constitution doesn't mention political parties. George Washington, our first president, was not elected in a national political contest. Instead, he was chosen unanimously by the electoral college (see page 28).

By the end of Washington's first four-year term, two strong political parties were developing. Over the years, other parties formed as people became unhappy with what they saw and heard in government. Each party tends to draw strong support from different regions of the country. Members of all the political parties have constantly challenged each other to step forward with new ideas and fresh solutions.

The Federalists

In the early days of the United States, men who believed in a strong national (federal) government joined the Federalist Party, organized by Alexander Hamilton. Members tended to be wealthy businessmen who valued strong economic ties with England. Federalist presidents were John Adams and John Quincy Adams.

The Democratic-Republicans

Men like Thomas Jefferson, who believed that state governments should be stronger than the central government, formed the Democratic-Republican Party. This party favored low government spending and appealed to farmers and southerners. Besides Jefferson, Democratic-Republican presidents were James Madison and James Monroe.

The Democratic Party

The Democratic Party is descended from Jefferson's Democratic-Republican Party. It became a national party in 1828 when Andrew Jackson was running for president. Small-scale farmers and city workers were attracted to this new party, which strongly favored social programs. Noted Democratic presidents have included Grover Cleveland, Lyndon B. Johnson, Franklin D. Roosevelt, and Bill Clinton.

The Whigs

Every party needs at least one opposing party — and the Whigs opposed Andrew Jackson's Democrats. The Whigs were organized in 1834 and named for the British Whigs. They believed in limited presidential power. But this party didn't survive the disputes that led up to the Civil War in 1861. Presidents William Henry Harrison and Zachary Taylor were Whigs.

The Republican Party

Formed in 1854, the Republican Party wanted to abolish slavery and fund a railroad across the country, among other things. Abraham Lincoln was the first Republican president. After the Civil War, the Republican Party helped rebuild the destroyed South and supported amendments to the Constitution that enabled more men to vote. Republican presidents have included Ulysses S. Grant, Theodore Roosevelt, Dwight D. Eisenhower, and Ronald Reagan.

Party members can have unusual ways of showing their support. In 2000, one Republican's obituary read "In lieu of flowers, vote Bush."

GRAND OLD PARTY?

Sometimes a Republican candidate is referred to as a "GOP candidate." GOP stands for Grand Old Party, a nickname for the Republicans since 1880. But even the Republican National Committee agrees that the Democratic Party is older!

Third, Fourth, Twelfth ... Parties

W hat if voters don't like either of the two main parties of the time? What if they don't feel these candidates are offering them what they want? Such disgruntled voters will turn elsewhere to vote for, or form, what is called a *third party*. This term is a bit confusing because there has often been more than one alternative to Democratic and Republican candidates on election ballots.

Third parties have a hard time getting on the ballots of every state. Sometimes, third-party supporters have to petition to get their candidates on the ballot. You may see the third-party candidate in the papers and on TV, but she may not appear on your state's ballot on Election Day.

No third-party candidate has ever become president. Theodore Roosevelt came closest in 1912, finishing in second place. But third parties have always kept the two major parties on their toes

and sometimes have greatly affected the election outcome. Votes expected to go to a Democratic candidate, for example, might be split between her and a third-party candidate (called a *spoiler* in this situation), and the Republican candidate wins.

Third parties campaign and have conventions just like the major parties (see page 36). Usually, they have very specific views that appeal to a rather limited part of the voting population, but they may still receive millions of votes.

For example, the National Prohibition Party (1872) didn't want any alcohol sold in the

United States. The Progressive Party (1912) supported women's suffrage and government reform. In the 2000 election, the Green Party appealed for a "global citizens'" movement of consumer groups and environmentalists.

Some of the third-party names have been very unusual: the Know-Nothing Party (1856), the Vegetarian Party (1948), and the Down with Lawyers Party (1980). The list of party names on a presidential ballot can be long — in 1988, there were candidates representing nineteen different parties.

WHO'S ON LEFT?

When you listen to people talking about politics, you'll hear them use the directions "left" and "right." What on Earth do these directions have to do with government?

Just before the French Revolution of 1789, King Louis XVI held meetings with French citizens. The nobles sat on the king's right at the table, while the priests and middle classes sat on his left. (You'll notice that the lower classes weren't represented at all — hence the Revolution!)

After the overthrow of King Louis, the government followed the same general pattern. Members who supported tradition sat on the right, and those who supported social equality sat on the left. Today, some people say that most Republicans are on the right, and Democrats are on the left. Although, just to confuse things, there can be left-leaning Republicans and right-leaning Democrats!

Primary Action

The U.S. Constitution calls for a presidential election every four years in November. Every race begins with a candidate's announcement that he is going to run for office. Usually, candidates tell their families first, then their political supporters, and finally the media and the public. Sometimes, they announce their candidacy more than a year before the election. (Presidential candidates often start running nearly four years before, right after the last election.) To qualify to be on ballots, candidates must usually gather a certain number of signatures from voters to show they have support.

Sometimes, more than one person in a party may decide she wants to represent the party in an election. But only *one* can run in the final race. The parties hold *primary elections* to narrow the field to their top candidate. These primary elections are held for nearly every level of office in government.

Most presidential primaries are held in the first six months of a presidential election year. Not every state holds a primary election, but those that do bring a lot of media attention to the candidates. A day in March is called "Super Tuesday" because of the number of primary elections held on that day.

If an *incumbent* (a person already holding the office) wants to return as president, other members of his party usually do not try to run against him. They would rather see him win the presidency a second time for their party.

There are primary elections for Democrats and separate primaries for Republicans. Voters cast a ballot in only one primary. At the same time as they vote for

their choice of candidate for the presidential race, voters can also select candidates for Senate and House of Representatives seats. State and local officials are also included on the ballot.

A *caucus* is a meeting held in some states instead of a primary election. Members of a party and party leaders decide who they want to be the party's nominee for president. Candidates for state and local elections can also be chosen at these caucuses.

At the end of all these elections and meetings, it's clear who the final presidential candidates will be — and the race is on!

The first big caucus is held in Iowa, a few weeks before the first primary election in New Hampshire, the site of the nation's first primary since the 1920s.

Building a Government

A *platform* tells voters what the party wants to do about problems facing America. A *plank* is a single item of the party's plan of action. Options for the homeless or increased funding for education might be two planks of a candidate's platform. Tax cuts and a re-examination of the country's military budget might be others. Candidates are free to diverge from the "official party platform."

It's difficult to argue with a candidate who says she wants less crime in our cities and wiser government spending. What candidate is going to say she wants more crime and reckless spending? You have to find out how candidates intend to carry out their platform.

"Platform" and "planks" remind us of the early days of campaigning when politicians stood on wooden platforms high above the crowds and delivered fiery speeches. Although today we may hear and see speeches on TV, we still have to listen and interpret what we hear just as carefully as our ancestors did.

Party Time!

Throughout the primary elections, everyone — the media, the voters, and the campaign workers — has been counting the number of delegates committed to each candidate.

Let's say Kitsy Reardon, a Democrat from Massachusetts, has received most of the Democratic votes in the primary elections. Likewise, Tony Perez, a Republican from Colorado, got the majority of the Republican support. In the summer before the presidential election, Kitsy and Tony expect to be formally nominated as their parties' candidates for the office of President of the United States. These nominations take place at huge meetings called *conventions*.

Nominating conventions have been held by major parties for nearly 170 years. All states and territories and the District of Columbia send delegates to nominate party candidates amid songs, cheers, parades, and thousands of balloons. Conventions look like a lot of fun on TV, but there's also lots of work to be done over just a few days. Delegates hear enthusiastic speeches from their leaders. They discuss and decide the party platform (see page 35). And they formally choose their nominees.

Some people argue that these days it's clear who the nominees will be *before* the conventions even begin, so the meetings are just a waste of money. However, for the millions of voters who watch even a part of the conventions on TV, they are a way to learn more about the nominees, their records, and their ideas. Conventions bring the upcoming election to life.

Alabama, Arkansas, Arizona ...

On the third day of the convention, one of Kitsy's supporters, with an enthusiastic speech, nominates her as the Democratic candidate for president. Someone else follows up with a seconding speech. Then it's time for the roll call.

The convention secretary calls the states alphabetically. When they hear their states called, delegation leaders go to a microphone and announce how many votes their states give to each candidate. When the votes are tallied, the official party nominee is named — Kitsy's made it! By this time, she's named her choice for vice president, and the party convention quickly ratifies that *running mate*. (Tony goes through the same process at the Republican convention — also held during the summer, but in a different city — to become *his* party's official candidate.)

The last day of the convention is the noisiest because that's when the nominees for president and vice president make their acceptance speeches. The presidential nominee gives the final speech. Kitsy and Tony try to use their speeches to get all the voters excited about the campaign weeks ahead. They want to inspire voters to get out and work for their parties — spreading the word about party platforms — to help them win the office of president.

There's been a great deal of hard work done by hundreds of people to get to this final night of the convention. There's no time for rest yet. A grueling election campaign is about to begin.

BARBIE'S ON BOARD

In 2000, the national nomination conventions had thousands of delegates cheering, carrying homemade posters, wearing crazy hats, and collecting stuff in goodie bags. One of the most popular items was "Delegate Barbie," a special edition of the doll made by Mattel. Bipartisan Barbie — a supporter of both parties — was dressed in a business suit and wore a convention ID badge. Representatives of the Smithsonian Institution asked delegates for items to add to the election displays in America's biggest museum. That means "Delegate Barbie" went to Washington, D.C. — but not as an elected official!

"Getting to Know You ..."

When Kitsy Reardon and Tony Perez announced their candidacies, you might never have heard of them. Why should you give either one your vote? How well do they work with other people? What do they say about the issues? How can you get more information about Kitsy and Tony?

Choosing a candidate can be difficult. Politicians from different parties often say basically the same thing. After all, candidates wouldn't say they don't care about the environment. Listen carefully, though. Kitsy may propose a quick, short-term solution. Tony may say the environment is not a top priority. The national debt is his main concern.

How do you find out what Kitsy and Tony stand for? Campaign literature is one way. Political parties print tons of material. Usually, these publications feature biographies of the candidates and outline key election issues.

Newspapers and TV stations assign reporters to cover each candidate. These reporters often file stories daily. Sometimes, they investigate the candidates' backgrounds. Sometimes, they analyze their positions or their campaigns. Some reporters have the job of finding unusual, often funny, information. For example, if either Kitsy or Tony *tries* to dance the "Charleston" with a local dignitary at a fund-raising dinner — and *slips* — we'll hear all about it, and probably see film footage!

With the help of a campaign manager and hundreds of paid and volunteer supporters, Kitsy and Tony will campaign until they're exhausted. They'll stroll through malls or down busy streets, shaking hands and chatting. They'll want to speak to as many voters as possible by Election Day. They'll ask what people are concerned about. And they'll try to have a ready answer to all the questions they're asked.

You may even get to talk to Kitsy or Tony face to face. Candidates visit neighborhoods across the country to talk with voters. At "town-hall meetings," they may take questions from the audience. Town-hall meetings remind us of how campaigning used to be done — a local candidate met with the voters in his community, and they felt they knew him. Usually, they did know him, perhaps since childhood!

By Election Day, Tony and Kitsy probably will be fighting off pounds after too much fast food or too many fund-raising banquets. Their arms will hurt from all the hand-shaking, and they may be sick of smiling so much. Kitsy may have dark circles under her eyes from missing sleep to give speeches.

A CANDIDATE ABROAD

In the 2000 presidential election, Green Party candidate Ralph Nader traveled to Canada to ask for the support of the half-million American voters living there. American citizens living in foreign countries can still be registered to vote in their last U.S. home. Imagine that your aunt teaches American history at a university in Canada. If she's a U.S. citizen, she could vote. So could her daughter, who could be an American citizen even if she was born in Canada and has never lived in the United States. Nader is believed to be the only American presidential candidate to have campaigned in a foreign country.

(In 2000, candidate George W. Bush brought a pillow from home so that he could sleep better during the campaign.) Tony's family may hardly recognize him because he's been away from home for so long. But it's all part of a candidate's life, and Kitsy and Tony hope that on Election Day their efforts will bring them victory.

The old saying "As Maine goes, so goes the nation" means that the candidate who wins the most presidential votes in Maine will be the next president. Hmmm. A look at the election results over the years proves that this isn't always the case!

Campaign Bits and Bites

Politicians know that TV is extremely useful during a presidential campaign. Not just for running political ads — daily news programs also help campaigners communicate with the public. TV networks send reporters on "special assignment" to follow the major candidates across the country, meeting and greeting their fellow Americans in the search for votes.

Voters who can't get out to actually meet the candidates can sit in their living rooms and catch up on the day's campaign events on the evening news. Campaign advisers plan occasions to be seen by as many voters as possible. You may hear some of these terms when you catch up on the day's events.

Photo op — an event set up for TV cameras and newspaper photographers. Remember Kitsy doing the "Charleston"? That was a photo op. So are flipping pancakes at a charity event, cutting the ribbon at a museum opening, trying on a new hat, and even the traditional kissing babies.

Sound bite — a short bit of a candidate's speech or her reply to an interviewer's question. A sound bite lasts only about fifteen seconds, so candidates have to be sure they get their point across clearly and quickly! Often, a news program will run sound bites from several candidates to summarize the day's events.

Message of the day — the candidate's theme for the day, such as education reform. The candidate spends the day visiting a school, reading a book to a class, and speaking with teachers and parents. The evening news will report this visit and what the candidate said. The next day, he will deliver another message to voters, focusing on another theme in another place.

PASS THE BANANA BREAD, PLEASE

During the months before the 2000 presidential election, then-vice president Al Gore began a "kitchen-table" campaign. For a while, he had breakfast with voters in swing states. He drank chai, an Asian tea beverage, with a voter in Oregon and discussed business with the owner of the chai business. Another day, he ate a cheeseburger-and-curly-fries lunch with students in a high school.

A very long day began in Ohio and took

Gore through four states! He slept that night on a sofa bed in a Maine home he'd never visited before. Before unfolding the sofa, he spent about two hours chatting and munching banana bread. The next day, Gore was traveling again.

"Kitchen-table" discussions give the candidate an idea of what matters to individual Americans — and provide a more casual, homey image for the media.

Spin — the angle or position taken on a certain campaign issue or event. Campaign workers usually speak with reporters and photographers before campaign events. As a result, they hope that reporters will relate the campaign events with a slant favorable to their candidate. Everyone wants to look good on the campaign trail, and spin can make even a candidate's bite of pie at a county fair look like a huge event.

"Can We Talk ...?"

Some states, such as Massachusetts and Virginia, are known as staunchly Democratic or Republican voting states. During a campaign, therefore, parties try to focus on other states where they know they have a chance of persuading voters to change their vote from one party to another. These targeted states are called *swing states* because voters can "swing" either way. Campaign

workers will, of course, want to spend more time and money in swing states that have the largest number of electoral college votes.

Have Slogan — Will Run

When you urge your school team on to victory at the hockey play-offs, you cheer, "Go get 'em, Melrose High!" or whatever your school is called. This slogan whips up team spirit. Election slogans work the same way. Here are some slogans from past elections.

★ **"Tippecanoe and Tyler, Too"** (1840 — William H. Harrison, "Tippecanoe" because of a battle he won there. John Tyler was his vice-presidential running mate.)

★ **"54–40 or Fight"** (1844 — James K. Polk, who wanted the United States to own western land up to the 54th parallel, 40 degrees, of latitude. After his election, Polk had to settle on the 49th parallel as the border with present-day Canada.)

★ **"Keep Cool with Coolidge"** (1924 — Calvin Coolidge)

★ **"I Like Ike"** (1952 — Dwight D. Eisenhower, nicknamed "Ike")

★ **"Experience Counts"** (1960 — Richard M. Nixon, already vice president)

★ **"All the Way with LBJ"** (1964 — Lyndon B. Johnson, known by his initials)

Notice that the name of the candidate is often part of the slogan. Some candidates today hire advertising agencies to create election slogans that will keep their names in voters' minds right until Election Day.

Collectibles with a Message

Some people collect campaign items from the past, showing how parties promoted candidates.

Promotional items appeared when Andrew Jackson was elected in 1828, but historians agree the election of William Henry Harrison in 1840 was the beginning of campaign materials like those we have today. At first, parties passed out silk ribbons and bandannas with the candidate's portrait or slogan on them. Eventually, political buttons became more popular.

The first buttons were made of tintypes, an early form of photography. Tin pins were first used in the 1880s. In 1896, celluloid, a plastic-like material, was invented and used for political buttons. Celluloid campaign material remained popular until the tin buttons, similar to those we wear now, became popular again in the 1920s. In 2000, one presidential candidate designed his own campaign button instead of using a team of hired artists. Al Gore sketched a red swoosh, a white star, and "Gore 2000" on a blue background — and

that's the futuristic design his supporters wore.

Bumper stickers for cars provided mobile political advertisements starting in the 1950s. A famous sticker for presidential nominee Barry Goldwater said "AuH_2O-64" — in other words, "Goldwater–1964," using the symbols for "gold" and "water" from the scientific periodic table.

Other campaign items have included hairbrushes displaying William Henry Harrison's face (1840), and tiny baby dolls made of soap labeled, "My papa will vote for McKinley" (1896). Torches with candidates' names provided light for nighttime parades from the 1850s to the 1890s. Postcards from the early 1900s had pictures of the candidates and plenty of patriotic decorations. Cigar bands had a portrait of Calvin Coolidge (1924), and Kennedy supporters wore Styrofoam "straw" hats (1960).

KEEP THE BALL ROLLING!

During the 1840 election, Harrison supporters made a huge ball out of leather, about ten feet in diameter, and covered it with political rhymes. Specially dressed boys rolled the "Great Ball" through the state of Maryland. Other Whig voters rolled slogan-covered, twine-and-paper "Harrison balls" in different towns in support of their candidate, singing campaign songs as they rolled along.

Pass the 'Lection Cake, Please!

In 1796, John Adams defeated Thomas Jefferson and served as president for one term. That same year, a recipe for Election Cake was published in America's first cookbook, *American Cookery*, by Amelia Simmons. Here's the list of ingredients.

30	quarts of flour
10	pounds of butter
14	pounds of sugar
12	pounds of raisins
3	dozen eggs
1	pint of wine
1	quart of brandy
4	ounces of cinnamon
4	ounces of fine ground coriander seed
3	ounces of ground allspice
1	quart of yeast milk

There aren't many directions given with the recipe — just mix the flour, milk (how much?), and yeast and let the mixture sit overnight. The next day, work the other ingredients into the dough and bake it. (No temperature or baking time is given.)

We're also not told how many voters this 90-pound "cake" would have served. And there was no frosting on this celebration treat!

More Wonderful Food

★ During the 1840 election, William Henry Harrison supporters built a log cabin (his symbol) in Albany and ate corn bread, cheese, and cider. In West Virginia, "Harrisonites" held a political rally for about 30,000 people. They served a meal that included 360 hams, 8,000 pounds of bread, and 4,500 pies for dessert.

★ One of Abraham Lincoln's favorite foods was an election cake baked by his wife, Mary Todd Lincoln. The Lincolns didn't add the wine to their recipe — but they plumped up the raisins in a little bit of brandy! And they did frost their cake with a sugary glaze.

★ In the late 1800s, "burgoo" was one of the most popular dishes served at political rallies in Kentucky. It was a thick, spicy stew of meat and lots of vegetables, such as corn and okra.

★ During the 1964 election, Lyndon B. Johnson liked to serve traditional barbecued meals to the Democratic campaign supporters who gathered at his ranch in Texas. The word "barbecue" comes from the Spanish word *barbacoa*, or "frame," like the frame that holds the food above the hot coals while cooking.

★ Kraft produced special Macaroni & Cheese Dinner boxes for delegates at the 1996 Republican and Democratic conventions. Each group got its symbol — elephant or donkey — dressed in a suit and standing in a shower of confetti.

★ During the 2000 election, you could find recipes posted on a Web site by Democrats and Republicans for "Tennessee Treats" (Gore) and "Texas Governor's Mansion Cowboy Cookies" (Bush). The Web site invited visitors who baked the sweets to "debate the issue that really matters" — taste!

The Race Is On

Traditionally, the public becomes more interested in a presidential election after Labor Day. Summer vacations are over (candidates often don't take a summer vacation but keep working), the national convention hoopla has faded, and everyone has a "back-to-school, back-to-work" feeling. Some party advisers think that voters don't really start paying attention to the upcoming election until after baseball's World Series is over in October!

If people aren't *really* listening until October, candidates and their workers have only about a month to get their attention, change their minds, and convince them to get out and vote. They study public opinion surveys closely. One day, Kitsy may be leading with five percent of the vote — that means Tony's workers will put more energy into their campaign. A week later, surveys might report that Kitsy's lead is gone. As the days go by, campaigns will spend more money to capture the attention of voters. In fact, tens of millions of dollars can be spent on advertising in just one year of electioneering.

Surveying the Situation

During an election campaign, you or someone in your family might be stopped on the street and asked if you'd like to take part in a public opinion survey, or poll. At first, you might be tempted to say you're too busy to answer questions. But such surveys are very important. They are one way you have to let the candidates and the government know what you think of them. Surveys can be very powerful tools for everyone concerned.

Realistically, pollsters (the people making the surveys) can't talk to *everyone* in America, so they select a cross section of people to speak with. The more people the pollsters talk to, the more accurate their results will be. But, because they only talk to a percentage of the population, surveys can never be totally accurate. That's why you'll hear about the "margin of error" when the results of the survey are made known to the public.

Campaign workers and the media hire pollsters to track how candidates are doing and which issues most interest the public. Sometimes, the results of the surveys don't "match" because of whom the pollsters talked to. For example, issues that mean a lot to America's young voters may not be as important to older people.

As Election Day draws near, more surveys are done. Campaign workers are looking for the undecided or swing voters they need to win. You'll hear new numbers and predictions every day once November arrives. Even on Election Day, the pollsters are busy with exit polls (see page 18). Some critics would like to see fewer surveys done, especially as people leave the polling places. The incomplete information about which candidate is ahead in the polls actually discourages some people from going to vote. They think the "winner" has already been decided, so why bother? Those looking at campaign reform are looking hard at how surveys are used and reported.

★★★ 47

Animal Farm

Listen to the radio and TV commentaries during an election and you might think you've stumbled into a barnyard. You'll hear about ducks, dogs, lambs, and horses. Here's a guide to who's who.

Underdog

During a campaign, pollsters often ask voters whom they plan to vote for. The results of these public opinion polls let people know who is in the lead before Election Day. The "underdog" is the candidate who seems to be losing. Just because a candidate is called the underdog a few weeks before Election Day doesn't mean he will lose the election. Voters can change their minds right up until they mark their ballots.

Dark Horse

Sometimes people believe a candidate has no chance at all of winning. Then on Election Day — surprise! In horse racing, the same thing happens. Most of the bets have been placed on, say, Gorgeous George, but Marvy Martha wins the race. The candidate who comes "from nowhere" like that and wins the election is the "dark horse."

During a campaign, reporters also use the horse-racing expression "running neck-and-neck." It means that candidates seem to be within a few votes of each other.

Sacrificial Lamb

If a very popular candidate is running for re-election, the chances of beating her may be slim. A candidate who runs against her is almost sure to lose, but a party may still recruit someone to run and speak up for its position. That candidate is a "sacrificial lamb."

Why be a sacrificial lamb? To gain experience, and perhaps be rewarded by the party with an appointment or support in another election.

Lame Duck

A president who announces he's retiring (or is unable to run for a third term because of the Twenty-Second Amendment) can expect to be called a "lame duck." He is still in power, but everyone knows he's on the way out. Voters don't pay as much attention to a politician in this position, so it's more difficult for him to get things done. Like a duck that can't fly, he can't make any progress. Voters are looking ahead to the next president, who they hope will give them what they want and need.

Pork Barreling

"Pork barreling" is when government members give funds or contracts to supporters — and their states — rather than to people who might be better qualified or more deserving. Sometimes, this is how sacrificial lambs are rewarded. ("Pork barreling" is also known as "the spoils system," in which loyal supporters are rewarded with jobs.)

LONG TRUNK ... OR LONG EARS?

Before TV and radio, political parties used printed materials to entice and educate voters. They adopted symbols to represent candidates or parties. For example, a log cabin printed on ribbons and signs in 1840 was meant to remind voters of William Henry Harrison's humble "of the people" roots. In its early years, the Democratic Party used the "wake up" image of a rooster as its party symbol. But a noisy rooster, puffing up his chest and preening, was probably not the best image to win votes.

Thanks to political cartoons in the late 1800s, the donkey became the accepted symbol of the Democrats and the elephant the official mascot of the Republicans. What do these animals mean? According to party documentation, "the Democrats think of the elephant as bungling, stupid, pompous, and conservative — but the Republicans think it is dignified, strong, and intelligent. On the other hand, the Republicans regard the donkey as stubborn, silly, and ridiculous — but the Democrats claim it is humble, homely, smart, courageous, and lovable."

You Say ... I Say ...

Debates are now an important event in every presidential election. During debates, a moderator will ask the candidates questions about important issues. Candidates study for such debates. They meet with their advisers and practice, the way you might practice for a question-and-answer session on a school research topic. Among other things, Kitsy's advisers will be checking how flashy her jewelry is in the studio lights. Often, candidates decide to wear red, white, and — what else? — blue.

Sometimes candidates meet for more than one televised debate, in different parts of the country. Debates can last for up to two hours. Candidates bring notes with them, but there isn't much time to refer to them — people want to see if a candidate "knows his stuff" without looking down at notes. Candidates' advisers don't want them looking *down* at all — they should be keeping their heads *up*, looking directly at their opponents and showing strength and conviction. Voters are watching "body language," not just listening. Tony will want to look friendly and a bit casual, but he doesn't want to go too far and look sloppy and unprofessional.

You might think it's easy to set up these political debates. It's not. It's hard work because advisers want everything about the debate to make their candidate look good. For example, they have to agree on the height of the speakers' lecterns — one candidate can't appear shorter (weaker?) than the other. (Good posture is also very important at a debate!) Even the room temperature can be an issue! But after all the quibbling is over, the debate takes place.

At the end of a debate, there's no official announcement of who won. Each side's advisers claim that their candidate won — or at least did better than expected. Other people discuss who really won, on the radio, on TV, and in regular conversations. But the only win that counts will come on Election Day.

As Simple as Black and White?

Televised debates have been part of our presidential campaigns since 1960, when John F. Kennedy and Richard M. Nixon used the "new" medium to reach seventy million voters. People who listened to the debate on the radio believed that Nixon had won, but TV viewers selected Kennedy as the winner. The reason? Kennedy "used" the medium well. His dark suit contrasted with the background. Nixon's gray suit blended into the set. Kennedy wore performer's makeup and looked young and healthy. Nixon refused the makeup for the first of their four debates, appeared unshaven, and perspired under the bright studio lamps. One candidate for the Oval Office looked strong and energetic; the other looked unhealthy and weak. More voters watched the first debate than the other three. Words plus image — whom would *you* have voted for?

TECH GLITZ

Political parties always try to use the latest technology to reach voters, and today that includes the Internet. Candidates set up Web sites to explain their positions, share their biographies, and announce their speaking and traveling schedules.

During the 2000 political conventions, people signed on as "dot-com delegates" and followed the proceedings on-line. Parties promised (and usually delivered) special e-mails about the issues, camera views from around the convention halls, and on-line news conferences. People using their computers to spread the word about voting were said to be "ringing cyber doorbells" to raise votes for their favorite candidates. In chat rooms and on message boards, voters debated issues and personalities.

"How Do I Look and Sound?"

When you apply for a job at a department store, you shouldn't wear dirty clothing and mumble — not if you hope to get the job. You should dress and act appropriately for success. First impressions are important in elections, too. Candidates spend lots of time and money "improving their images" before meeting voters.

Tony and Kitsy might wear denim jeans and shirts with the sleeves rolled up while campaigning on college campuses or visiting county fairs. But to speak at town-hall meetings and on TV, they'll wear business suits, exchanging their denim and earth-toned clothing for plenty of navy, white, and red.

Candidates who "look bad" on TV hire media experts to groom them for public appearances. Some candidates get complete makeovers, everything from a new hairstyle and contact lenses to a snappier wardrobe. Consultants might even help candidates modify how they pronounce words. If Kitsy has a Boston accent, people in New England may not care — in fact, they may identify her as "one of us." But elsewhere in the country, voters might not understand Kitsy's speech, or like it.

Candidates have to walk a fine line between too formal and too casual. And if voters start to believe a candidate is playing a part instead of being sincere, they usually resent all the image polishing.

"Three, Two, One ... You're On!"

Televised debates and radio interviews have long been part of presidential campaigns, but in recent elections, candidates have used popular TV programs to reach more voters.

During the 2000 election, candidates George W. Bush and Al Gore both appeared on talk shows. About twenty-two million viewers watch the daytime program *Oprah* — a lot of voters! The candidates traded jokes with hosts such as David Letterman and Regis Philbin. Gore even played himself on the cartoon *Futurama*. Other presidents have used similar programs to gather votes. Richard Nixon appeared on the 1968 comedy show *Laugh-In*, and Bill Clinton played the saxophone on late-night TV in 1992.

Campaign advisers like TV-show guest shots. They say that the public can see more of the candidate's personality, sense of humor, and family life on these shows than on the campaign trail. Show biz plus politics equals votes.

Funny Faces

Sometimes, thanks to cartoonists, one part of a candidate's face becomes his trademark. President Teddy Roosevelt was noted for his bushy mustache, and Jimmy Carter for his huge grin. Political cartoonists liven up newspaper editorial pages with their funny, but meaningful, comments on politicians. Their caricatures exaggerate a candidate's facial features and can replace the real image of the person in people's minds.

Political cartooning has been going on for thousands of years. Europe's kings and queens, even Egypt's pharaohs, have been caricatured. From the 1800s until today, most caricatures have been found in magazines and newspapers.

One of America's most famous political cartoonists was Thomas Nast (1840–1902). He drew pictures for *Harper's Weekly* from 1862 until 1886. He helped Ulysses S. Grant win the presidency in 1872 by attacking opponents with his "nasty" cartoons. (Nast also drew the Republican elephant, the Democratic donkey, and some of the earliest portraits of Santa Claus with his sack of toys.)

During the 2000 election, cartoonists drew George W. Bush's ears as huge and his eyes as tiny. They poked fun at Al Gore's stiff mannerisms. Check out the editorial page of *your* local paper — and be prepared to chuckle at, and think about, what the cartoonist has drawn for the day.

Run for the Money

It takes a lot of money to run a campaign. Offices, cars, planes, and hotel rooms are rented. Assistants are paid. There are printing costs and huge payments for media ads. Volunteer supporters do a great deal of work, but a political party still needs a tremendous amount in its "campaign chest."

Campaign spending presents voters with issues to consider. What happens if a wealthy candidate runs against a poor one? Does the wealthy one have a better chance of winning because she can buy more media ads? How much personal money should candidates be able to spend? Should all contributions and media space be divided equally among all candidates?

Some people feel that individuals or businesses that give large donations will be "rewarded" if that candidate wins. They might get special access to the president or other officials, or even receive special favors. Reformers worry that ordinary voters feel their voices aren't heard because they can't afford to make huge donations. Contributions and their use are hotly debated issues.

Expensive Chicken Dinners

Candidates give speeches and meet voters, but they also have to raise money for their campaigns and their parties. They contact potential donors by phone and attend many fund-raising events, such as dinners where people may pay $2,000 or more for their meal — that must be some chicken! — and the chance to meet the candidate. Hollywood celebrities may come to entertain the donors. The media take photos and run stories. Presto! — more publicity and maybe more votes.

Business executives and lobbyists also collect record-breaking amounts of money at campaign banquets. Would you believe over twenty-five million dollars were raised at *one* gala during the 2000 election? Such large amounts of money worry reformers who want all voters, not just wealthy executives and entertainers, to feel they are part of the election process.

You Need *More* Money?

Political Action Committees (PACs) are another source of money before, during, and after elections. Since the mid-1900s, corporations, unions, and associations with common interests have formed these organizations to support candidates. Members donate money to their PAC, which can then pass it on to candidates who support the issues that interest those members.

Some PACs represent large groups, such as the Friends of the Earth. The Friends of the Earth PAC may give money to a candidate who promises to work for effective controls on how factories treat chemical waste. PACs usually take their names from the causes or people they claim to represent, such as Black America's PAC and the Women under Forty PAC.

PACs don't spend all their time collecting and distributing funds. They also run education programs, produce newsletters to tell members about proposed new laws, and maintain Web sites. They hire lobbyists to talk to legislators about their causes. (*Lobbyists* got their name because they wait in the lobbies or halls of government buildings, hoping to speak with lawmakers.)

PACs must file reports with the federal government explaining where they get their funding, and what they do with it. Federal law limits the amount of money each candidate can receive per election from PACs. But there's no limit on how much PACs can spend to help a candidate, providing they do not work with his campaign organization. Some campaign-finance reformers are upset by this.

Watch Out for Ms. Krime!

In most groups, there are people who decide to disregard the rules and do their own thing. Maybe Kal takes two Cokes when he's been told to have one. Maybe Katya looks at your paper during a math exam. They don't think they're hurting anyone, but the rules are there for a reason. If people take two Cokes, there won't be enough for everyone else. If Katya gets a high test score, and the marks are put on a curve, your grade may be lower than it would have been. And you've been cheated!

Fraud (cheating) can take place during elections, too. No one likes to admit it does, but it does. Close monitoring by election officials keeps fraud in check. But some people, like Ms. Krime, are very determined to do whatever it takes to get their candidate elected. Here are some of her election felonies.

Vote buying — Ms. Krime, with more money than brains, offers John Doe a few dollars to vote for her candidate. This is an expensive fraud, because Ms. Krime has to supply money or goods for every vote she wants. And with a secret ballot, how will Ms. Krime know if the paid voters *really* did vote for her candidate?

Multiple voting — Ms. Krime votes more than once in the election. She might do this by registering in two places, or sending a ballot by mail while voting in person. Or she might commit *false swearing* or *impersonation*. Heavily disguised (she thinks she's an actor!), Ms. Krime goes to the polling place pretending to be registered voter Mrs. Jones.

Ineligible voter — Ms. Krime's friend from Canada claims he's a U.S. citizen and registers to vote.

All election code violations are crimes, punishable by fines or time in prison. State and federal government officials are promoting a "zero tolerance" policy on any kind of voter fraud. Some states have "voter fraud hotlines," so concerned citizens can report suspected fraud. Watch out, Ms. Krime!

The Money Monitors

Today, most election-related crimes don't actually involve voting. Instead, they relate to raising and spending funds. And the agency responsible for spotting and punishing those crimes is the Federal Election Commission (FEC).

The FEC, created by Congress in 1975, watches over federal elections. The Commission's six members are appointed by the president and confirmed by the Senate. By law, no more than three Commissioners can be members of the same party, and four must vote together to make changes. These rules ensure that the FEC is nonpartisan.

The Commissioners are a busy bunch! The FEC's job starts with giving money to candidates with enough

support to qualify for public financing. Using money that taxpayers have designated, the FEC matches the dollars that each candidate raises from donations. In exchange for these *matching funds*, candidates agree to follow rules about how they collect and spend money. They can take only a limited amount from each donor, and must report every donation to the FEC. There's also a limit on how much candidates can spend overall.

But other groups can spend money to help candidates who are close to their limits. Both the Democratic and Republican parties run *issue ads*, which are supposed to educate the public about topics such as education or medical care. But often issue ads are made to help or hurt a specific candidate.

If the FEC finds that a candidate or party hasn't followed the rules, it can impose a fine — but by then the election is usually long over.

Election Day at Last!

Months of work have gone into the election, but at last it's the Tuesday after the first Monday in November. Election Day!

In every precinct, the polling places are ready. Opening times differ from state to state, but evening hours make it possible for people to vote on the way home from work or after supper. Let's imagine you're a first-time voter. You may be surprised at how simple the voting procedure is!

How will you recognize a polling place? The building will be announced in local newspapers and marked with signs. Outside the building, you'll probably see people holding placards for their candidates. They're hoping to influence your vote. But rules keep campaign literature and party supporters from being too near the entrance to a polling place so that no one will harass you as you go in to vote.

As you enter the polling place, you'll see election workers sitting behind a table. One will ask for your name and address, and check to see if it is on the list of registered voters. If it is, you may be asked to sign your name on the line with that information, or the worker may simply check your name off. That ensures no one else can pretend to be you and vote. You'll be handed a ballot or directed to a voting machine. (See page 16 for more about voting methods.) In the privacy of the voting booth, you can make your secret choice of candidates.

It might sound a bit confusing, but it really isn't. Everyone working at the poll is there to help you. Congratulations! You've just finished voting for the first time! You've made your mark and let your voice be heard.

Keeping an Eye on Things

When you enter the polling precinct, you may see some people who aren't just voting and leaving. These people are the *poll watchers*. Watchers, or observers, are trained volunteers from political parties, civic organizations, or groups such as the League of Women Voters. Their job is to observe all that happens on Election Day in the polling place. They might see someone trying to vote twice.

They might see a person too young to vote attempting to get a ballot. If they observe any actions that break election laws, they notify the inspector in charge.

Watchers keep an eye on the election workers, too. The workers must remain nonpartisan and fair throughout Election Day. Watchers can observe the counting of the ballots after the polls close. But a watcher cannot question any voter about her choice of candidate, or try to influence a voter's decision.

Thanks to the Internet, you can send a colorful, active, and noisy *e-card* to remind a friend to vote on Election Day.

YOU AT THE POLLS?

Are you interested in politics? Perhaps you're thinking about a career as a politician. You're sixteen and you already have a job at Ye Olde Candy Shoppe, so you're certainly old enough to work at a poll on Election Day, right?

In some states, you can work at the polls. In California, for example, if you are sixteen and a U.S. citizen, have a certain grade-point average, and help out around your school or community, you may be just what election officials are looking for. But before Election Day, you'll have to attend training classes. Although only one or two students may actually be needed at the polls, the training is a great opportunity to see up close how a poll works.

We Won!

Everyone has worked hard to win on Election Day. Unfortunately, some candidates lose their races. The winners, like Kitsy Reardon, are soon in their state or federal offices, surrounded by aides and getting used to their new schedules. The losing candidates, like Tony Perez, keep busy, too. Some take time off to rest after the hard campaign but then get back to work. Some begin making plans to run again.

There will be another election in a few years. Voters may become unhappy with the winners over the term, and the party that lost the last election may win the next one. Radio programs and newspapers will start "talking elections." And your TV programs will be interrupted again. The excitement of an election will be all around you — again.

There's always hope and opportunities for change in a democracy. There's always the next election when you can voice your opinion by voting — or maybe by running for office yourself!

The Gallery of Also-Rans

In 1965, an interesting museum opened on the mezzanine level of the First State Bank in Norton, Kansas (population 3,017). Local banker W.W. Rouse thought it would be nice to pay tribute to the "also-rans," the candidates who came in second in U.S. presidential elections.

Around the balcony walls are the framed, official Library of Congress portraits of all these people, including Samuel J. Tilden (who lost to Rutherford B. Hayes), Alfred E. Smith (who lost to Herbert Hoover), and, after the last election, Al Gore (who lost to George W. Bush). Beneath each portrait is a brief biography of the candidate. Even presidents like Jimmy Carter and George H. W. Bush went up on the wall after they lost their bids for re-election.

Stop by the museum the next time you're in Norton, Kansas.

Tony Perez

Glossary

acclamation: when only one candidate files a nomination paper, she is the winner by acclamation, or "popular acclaim"

advance polls: polling stations open before Election Day for voters who need to cast their ballots early

ballot: an electronic or printed form used to vote

campaign manager: the person who oversees a candidate's election plan and manages the details of the campaign

caricature: a portrait in which a person's features are deliberately exaggerated or distorted

concession: a candidate's acknowledgment after an election that the other side has won

constituents: voters in an electoral district who are represented by an elected official

delegate: a person who is selected to act on behalf of others at a convention

democracy: government by the people, either directly or through elected representatives

disenfranchisement: occurs when the right to vote is taken away

election day: the first Tuesday after the first Monday in November for the presidential election

electoral college: the 573 people (electors) chosen by the people of each state and the District of Columbia who cast the official votes for president

executive branch: the branch of the government headed by the president, which enforces laws

exit poll: a survey taken for news organizations of voters as they leave their polling places on Election Day to provide early information about how they voted

franchise: the right or privilege to vote; also called *suffrage*

incumbent: a person who is already holding a political office

judicial branch: the branch of the government that interprets the laws and includes the Supreme Court

landslide: an overwhelming political victory

legislative branch: the branch of the government that makes the laws for the country

nominate: to propose a candidate for a political office

nonpartisan: not influenced by and not supporting a political party

opinion poll: a survey of people to learn what they think about different candidates or issues

platform: a candidate's or a party's list of plans and promises

poll clerk: an official at a polling place

polling place: the place where voters cast their ballots; also called "the polls"

primary: an election among members of the same party who wish to be their party's candidate

ratify: a vote to make something official, such as a constitutional amendment or treaty

recount: the re-tabulation of votes in a close election

registration: signing up to vote

run-off election: a second round of voting between the two leading candidates; ensures the winner is the choice of over 50 percent of the voters

slogan: an election cheer that sums up what the candidate or party is saying and helps whip up interest and excitement

special election: an election scheduled between regular elections to choose a replacement for an official who has died or left office

suffragette: a woman who speaks out and battles for the right to vote

third party: a political party that is an alternative to the two major parties

Index